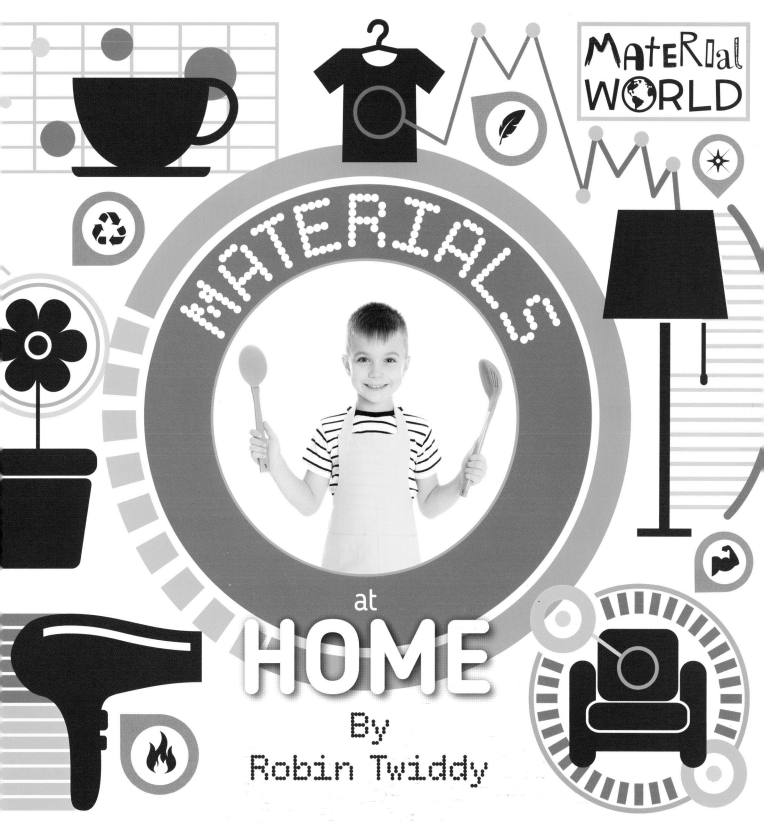

MATERIAL WORLD

MATERIALS

at

HOME

By
Robin Twiddy

BookLife
PUBLISHING

©2019
BookLife Publishing
King's Lynn
Norfolk PE30 4LS
All rights reserved.
Printed in Malaysia.

A catalogue record for this book
is available from the British Library.

ISBN: 978-1-78637-444-8

Written by:
Robin Twiddy

Edited by:
Kirsty Holmes

Designed by:
Danielle Jones

IMAGE CREDITS

Cover – Africa Studio. 1 & throughout – stuckmotion,1000 Words. 7 – ArTDi101. 8 – Yolanta. 9 – sichkarenko.com, Bilanol. 10 – Andrey_Popov. 11 – Ph.wittaya. 12 – karamysh. 13 – janniwet. 14 – Photographee.eu. 15 – Antonio Gravante. 16 – Photographee.eu. 17 – WIJI. 18 – trekandshoot. 19 – PONGPIPAT.SRi. 20 – Photographee.eu. 21 – Stanislav71. 22 – Kolbakova Olga. 23 – Anja W, Gearstd, Rakic. Images are courtesy of Shutterstock.com. With thanks to Getty Images, Thinkstock Photo and iStockphoto.

CONTENTS

Words that look like <u>this</u> can be found in the glossary on page 24.

WE'RE LIVING
IN A MATERIAL WORLD

Have you ever thought about what things are made of? Everything around you is made of something: wood, paper, plastic, glass... These things are called materials.

Houses, and everything in them, are made using materials.

All materials have <u>properties</u>. We can describe a material using its properties, such as how hard or soft it is.

Let's have a look at the materials in your home.

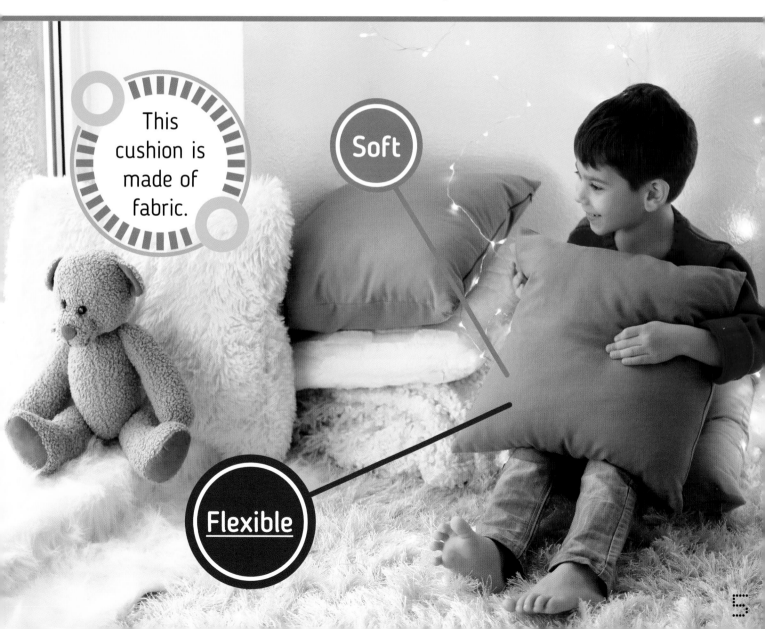

This cushion is made of fabric.

Soft

Flexible

A MATERIAL HOME

Think about your house. What materials do you think were used to build it? A lot of houses are made from bricks and mortar.

Brick
Wall

The mortar is wet when it is put on the bricks, then dries hard.

The mortar sticks the bricks together. When lots of bricks are stuck together with mortar, they make a wall. Brick walls are very strong.

FACT FILE: MORTAR
- 💧 Starts Wet
- 💎 Dries Hard
- 📏 Rough

FACT FILE: BRICKS
- 📏 Rough
- 💎 Hard
- 🪜 Rigid

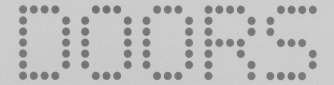

DOORS

What material is this door made of? Let's have a closer look.

The door is made of wood and glass. There are lots of different types of wood.

FACT FILE: WOOD

⬥ Hard

⬢ Smooth

💪 Strong

🌊 Floats in Water

FACT FILE: GLASS

⬥ Hard

⬢ Smooth

🪟 <u>Transparent</u>

FAMILY ROOM

Look in the family room. Can you find something made of plastic?

That's right! The television is made of plastic.

The outside of the television is made of plastic. Plastic is a <u>man-made</u> material. It can be made into any shape, colour or <u>texture</u>.

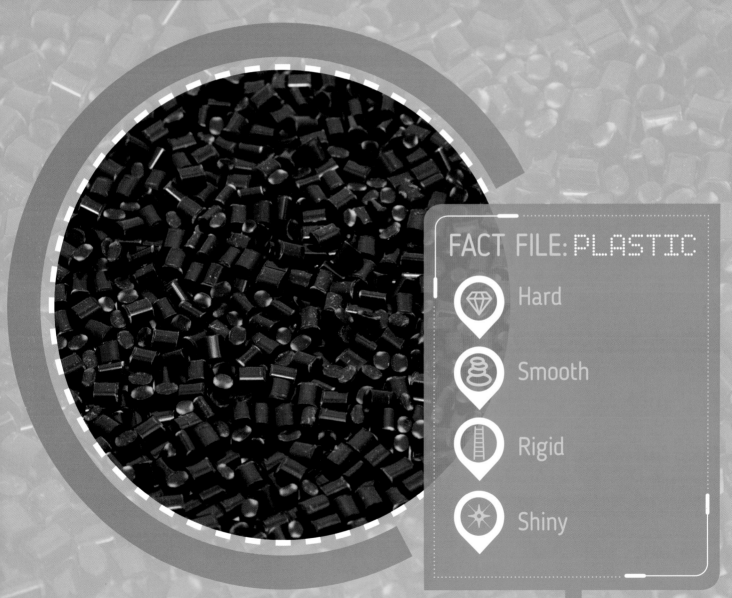

FACT FILE: PLASTIC

Hard

Smooth

Rigid

Shiny

Can you find something metal in this kitchen?

Kitchen Sink

Good work! You found the kitchen sink. This kitchen sink is made out of metal.

The kitchen sink is made from stainless steel, a type of metal. Metal is a good material for a sink because it is waterproof.

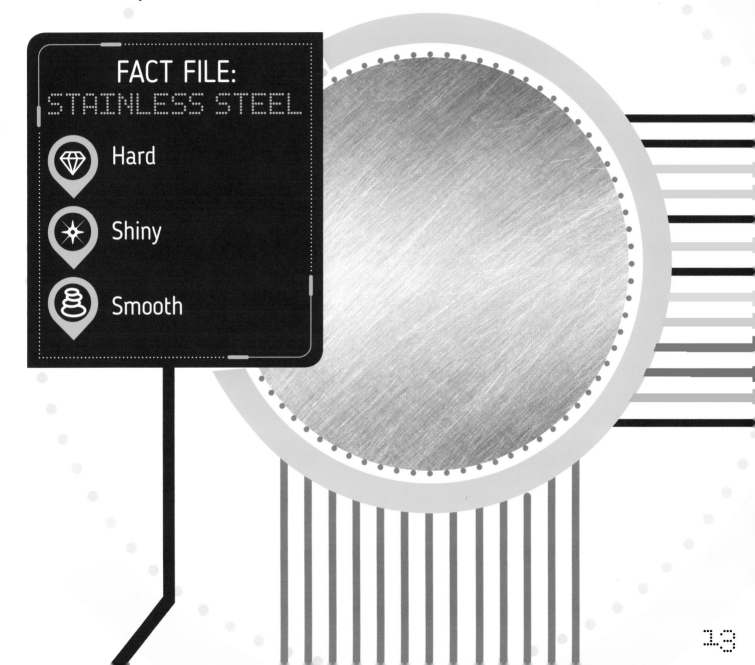

FACT FILE:
STAINLESS STEEL

Hard

Shiny

Smooth

BATHROOM

What is the toilet made of?

Porcelain is sometimes called china.

It is made from porcelain (say: por-ser-lin).

Porcelain is special type of clay that has been made hard by being heated in a <u>kiln</u>. Porcelain is used to make toilets because it is easy to clean.

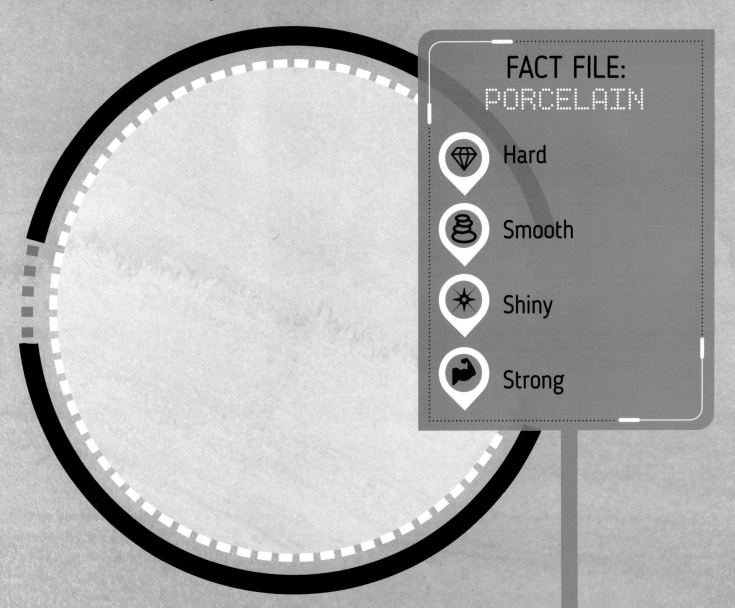

FACT FILE:
PORCELAIN

Hard

Smooth

Shiny

Strong

BEDROOM

Can you find something soft and warm in the bedroom?

Maybe you have a blanket or a quilt on your bed.

That's right – the bed cover is soft and warm! Bed covers are sometimes called duvets (say: doo-vays).

Duvets are made of a material called fabric. Fabric is made from lots of small criss-crossing <u>fibres</u>.

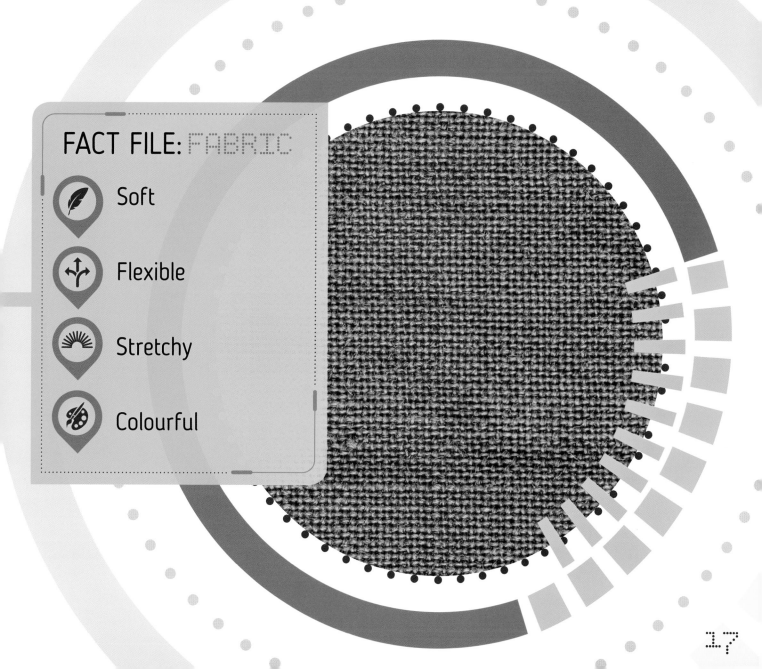

FACT FILE: FABRIC

- Soft
- Flexible
- Stretchy
- Colourful

GARAGE

What material do you think the floor in this garage is made of?

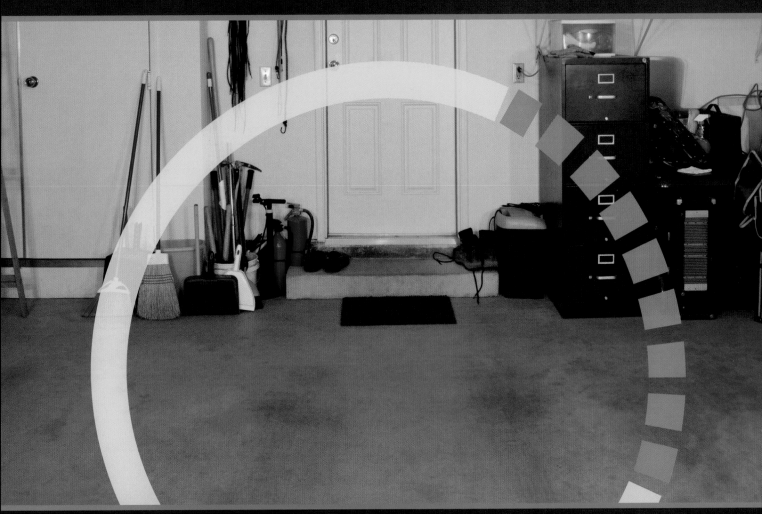

It is made from concrete.

Cement is a powder that is mixed with water to make a <u>liquid</u>. This liquid becomes concrete when it dries. This means that it keeps its shape.

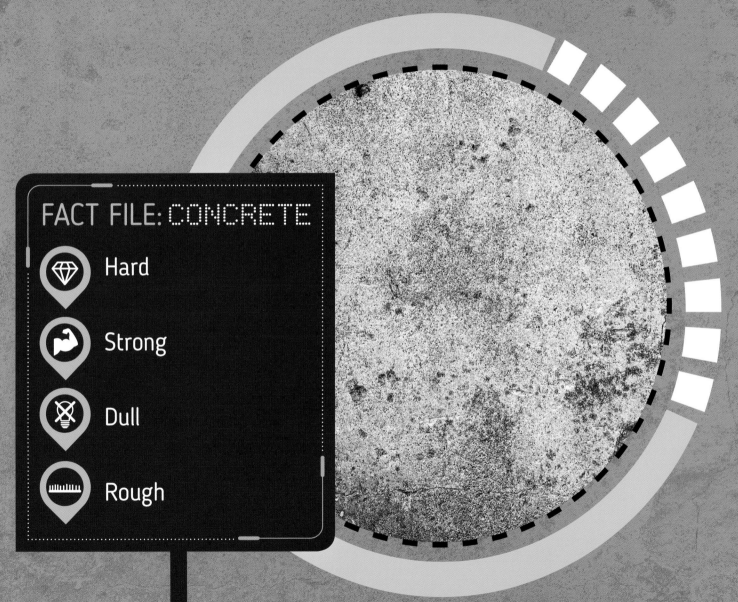

FACT FILE: CONCRETE

Hard

Strong

Dull

Rough

WALLS

Are the walls in your house covered with anything? Some walls are covered with paint and some are covered with wallpaper.

Wallpaper can have all sorts of fun colours and shapes on it.

#NIGHT NIGHT

Wallpaper is thick paper, much thicker than your drawing paper. Often, it has a <u>pattern</u> or colour printed on it.

FACT FILE:
WALLPAPER

Can Be Bumpy or Smooth

Can Be Torn

<u>Porous</u>

Flexible

MATERIAL MAGIC

Did you notice that some of the materials start as one thing and become another? When materials change, their properties change too.

Metals and plastics can change from rigid to flexible when they get hot.

IN YOUR HOME

Can you find any materials around your home that have some of the following properties:

Porous
Shiny
Smooth
Soft
Rough
Squishy
Hard

fibres	things that are like threads
flexible	easy to bend
kiln	a very hot oven for baking materials in
liquid	a material that flows, such as water
man-made	not natural: made by humans
pattern	a design with repeated parts
porous	able to soak up liquid
properties	ways of describing a material
rigid	difficult or impossible to bend
texture	the way something feels to touch
transparent	a material that lets light pass through it, causing it to be see-through

INDEX